Life Lines

Onam Priyadarshi

BookLeaf
Publishing
India | USA | UK

Presentation by *BookLeaf Publishing*

Web: www.bookleafpub.com

E-mail: info@bookleafpub.com

ISBN: 9789363318038

First edition 2024

I dedicate this book to my father,

Anshuman Priyadarshi.

Dear Daddy,

Just like you, I am a born poet.

Hope my writing makes you proud.

Love,

Queenie

ACKNOWLEDGEMENT

I would like to thank my mother, Veena Singh Priyadarshi, for always inspiring me to challenge the status quo.

Lots of hugs to my husband, Akashdeep Srivastava, for always nudging me to dream on.

Most importantly, lots of sloppy kisses to my baby, Yatika, for keeping me awake through countless nights so that I could think of these poems—my Lifelines.

And last but not least, gratitude and thanks to my family, friends and colleagues who have always encouraged me with a word of appreciation, be it for my actions or my words.

PREFACE

Ever since I started writing, the best expression I found for my feelings was through poetry.

At every milestone of life, be it a moment of joy, a personal loss, a pensive afternoon in the verandah just soaking in some peace or some marvellous observation, I have over the years spilled my heart out in these poems.

The beauty of these works is the clear evolution that one can see in the writing, thoughts and expressions ranging from that of a young adult to a mature thinker. It's almost a timelapse of my life as a writer spanning across the last eighteen years.

Hope some of it is relatable and all of it is loved.

Table of Contents

'Teening'

Santa's Christmas gift

In this season of gifts galore,
When all is merry like never before,
it's joy, dear children, I will give,
as memories that you can always relive.

In this season of togetherness and more,
When loneliness seems to have no cure,
it's love, dear people, that I will give,
so that the past, you can forget and forgive.

In this season of hatred and war,
When all is glum and ties are sore,
it's peace, dear world, that I will give,
so that you can live and let live.

An Oath of Friendship

First of August, Friendship Day,
It comes along each year this way.
Old pals and friends, all around
Close as they are, strongly bound.
To them today, I dedicate,
To every friend, yes, every mate.
An oath of friendship that one must take,
not just for friends, for friendship's sake.
"Friends we are and friends we'll be,
whatever may come till eternity,
forget me not and will not I,
As the years go by and by."

Love Conquers All

Ever since we were kids they taught us to be kind,
To respect every view but also have a strong mind.
To help everyone in need whether rich or poor,
To share and care in every way—less or more.

The hallowed portals that made our hearts truly sacred,
Have taught us to grow with love and get over any hatred.
That our words are knowledge and our actions are power,
And on those who are good at both, He will his blessings shower.

Today we are confident and conscientious leaders,
All thanks to the values and efforts of our teachers.
They saw each one of us as equal but also unique,
And taught us that hard work will conquer every peak.
That perfection is the key to stand out in a crowd,
And our humility when we do well will always make them proud.

Gratitude for everything we have learnt—big or small.
For school is still our beacon in life—whether we rise or we fall.

मन

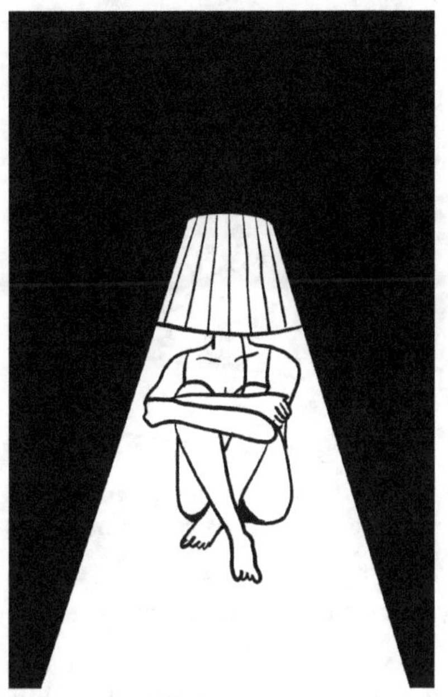

जीवन में कुछ बनना है तो,
मन को अपने बस में कर लो,
मन जो तुम्हारी बात सुनेगा,
जो तुम कहो वही करेगा,
तुम्हारा विकास हो कर ही रहेगा।
मन से मोह है, मन ही माया,
कहीं धूप है, कहीं है छाया।
मन ने जाल में जिसको फंसाया,
मुश्किलों से निकल है पाया।
मन को दोस्त है जिसने बनाया,
उसकी समझो पलटी काया।

Just Good Friends

Our eyes meet from across the classroom and we
quickly look away,
We leave a chit on the desk for each other every
day,
Something flutters in the stomach and the heart
skips a beat,
The cheeks are flushed, the words are rushed,
every time we meet.
We check our phones and just one smiley from
them makes us fine,
For hours we stare at the last chat wondering
when they will be online.
And when we see them typing, we can't wait to
see the text,
From then on we chat the whole night and can't
wait for the next.

We don't know what exactly, but it's a warm,
fuzzy feeling,
It could keep us smiling for hours staring at the
ceiling.
The heart asks us if we know what makes it so
different,
The brain declares it's nothing but the fact that
we're just good friends.

Love Loyola

The boards got over and hardly did I realize
'Twas the last time I was wearing my uniform,
For the last time were we addressed by father on
the same raised platform.
I turned around to discuss the paper with all my
mates,
And within minutes we were all diverging
through the school gates.
It was as if I was crossing,
A dreaded threshold,
To enter the world all alone,
To be strong and to be bold.
How unceremonious my exit was as my entry
had been in this school,
Where the days spent and the moments were
simply wonderful.
All those instances of pure joy
I'd like to relive,

And to all things that matter,
I'd have a message to give.

Each and every day spent here
Was full of life and fun,
I wish my journey had not ended
But only just begun.
To every person who made a difference just by
mere presence,
To every bough that gives the premises, the
distinct homely fragrance.
To the red stage which gives pale yellow a
striking dash of colour,
To the corridors where we witnessed astounding
acts of valour.
To the statue in the middle of the triangle, all I'd
like to say,
'It's because of you that our school is and will
always be this way.'
The classroom, the classes and the time that
Together we spent before,
Friends and teachers who I'll miss forever and
more.
I just wish they could all come back but I know
that's not about to be,
And all I have to depend on, is this fragment of
memory.

However if you feel the same, a stinging sense of nostalgia,
it's because more than everything else you'll always 'LOVE LOYOLA!'

Moody Foodie

Food is my guilty pleasure,
Comfort in all forms beyond measure.
There is some food for every mood,
To help you dance or cheer or brood.

Low calls for chocolate,
Lowest for cake,
And the darkest times call for an Oreo Shake.

A joyful evening is with jalebi and samosa,
Ain't no chatty breakfast without a masala dosa.
The party mood begins with the OG chicken
tikka,
Moving to chilli chicken with gravy while the
noodles' hakka.

And when the home is festive, there is puri and
kheer,
For the veggie times some form of exotic paneer.
But the SOS is when you're down with a cold,
Nothing beats the cozy chicken soup for the
soul.

And when you're exhausted, after hours of
stress,
All you need is rice and dal in a flavourful mess.

Welcoming the weekend with the Friday special
pizza,
Movie nights replete with biryani and raita,
The catching up with friends with some cheesy
fries,
The gossip adding on to the sizzler with spice.

So every time you wonder what's going to set
you right,
Think of your craving and your next bite.
Don't eat to live but love to eat,
Wherever your mood and food decide to meet.

'The Young Adult'

शर्माजी का बेटा

होनहार बिरवान के होत चीकने पात,
लाखों में एक है वो, अलग है उसकी बात,
कठिन परिश्रम से सींची है उसने परिवार की डाली,
उसकी उन्नति से होती है आंगन में हरदम हरियाली।

बड़ों की इज़्ज़त करता है वो और छोटों से प्यार,
चुनौतियों के आगे वो कभी ना माने हार।
उस्के कारण बाकी सब ने खूब खाये हैं डंडे,
हर परीक्षा, हर क्षेत्र में उसने गाड़े हैं झंडे।

है बुद्धिमान, गुणवान, संस्कारी और है सक्षम,
कितना भी चाहे कोई, उसका तेज नहीं हुआ कम।
कुछ लोग तो कहते हैं कि उसमें स्वयं राम ही बसते हैं,
जो उसके जैसे बन ना पाए वो इस बात पर हंसते हैं।

सबके लिए उदाहरण, उसके यश के किस्से कमाल हैं,
विश्व भर में उसके नाम के चर्चे बेमिसाल हैं।
सबको है उसपर गर्व, सबकी आँखों का है तारा,
और सबसे शान से शर्माजी कहते हैं—"यह बेटा है
हमारा।"

Love is Life

Be it gruesome war or a petty strife,
Life is love and love is life.
Be it the morning newspaper and the cup of tea,
Be it my grandma resting her weary knee.
Between a lovely maiden and her ardent lover,
Between an author and her first book's cover.
Between the newborn baby and the anxious
mother,
Between the chirpy sister and the doting brother.
Between an ageing father and his grown-up son,
Between the gunshot and one whose race has
just begun.
Between the limping forward and the lush green
field,

Between the winning team and the gleaming
shield.
Between the tearing father and the glowing
bride,
Between the beaming groom and his best man
beside.
Between the nation's flag and the dying soldier,
Each moment every breath growing colder,
With tears in his eyes and thoughts in his mind,
Of the love and the people he is leaving behind.
Between a seasoned chef and his favourite knife,
Between a smiling husband and his nagging
wife.
Be it gruesome war or a petty strife,
Life is love and love is life.

Why?

Why is it that the shower knob is always tough
to move?
Why is it that the people on the streets seem
happier than those in plush houses?
Why is war sometimes needed for peace?
Why is love overrated while maturity remains a
choice?
Why does a baby's smile make one forget all
woes?
Why is experience always needed while wisdom
seldom heeded?
Why is the softest person given the hardest
time?

Why is there light only at the end of the tunnel
while you need it to go through the dark?
Why is the why more important than the what
and the how?

Tintintara

वो पहली बार आया, तो था बहुत घबराया,
घर में लाके सबसे पहले उसको हमने सेरेलैक खिलाया,
छोटा था पर सुनता था वो हर बात हमारी,
बस बाहर जाने के लिए हमेशा थी तयारी।

धीरे-धीरे वही छोटू अब बन गए हैं शेर,
लोगों से भी ज़्यादा, इनके नखरे हैं ढेर,
हाथ से इनको कौर-कौर करके खिलाया जाता है,
घूमने के लिए खिलौनों को भी ले जाया जाता है।

छिपकली को देख के ये गोदी में चढ़ जाता है,
और बाहर कोई तो इनको खुंखार बुलाता है,
Daddy का चहेता है ये उनको खूब नचाता है,
जो वो बाहर जाएँ तो हमेशा मुँह लटकाता है,
Mummy का है फैन उनके साथ ही हरदम रहता है,
और मम्मी के ऊपर ही भरोसा करके सीढ़ी चढता है।

बिजली, बारिश और पटाखों से हम इसको बचाते हैं,
सुबह की चाय के साथ भौंक कर ये breaking news
सुनाते हैं,
सबको प्यार करता है और सबको है ये प्यारा,
Cutie hai, beauty hai, apna Tinoo Tintintara.

Ambi-social

Have you ever wondered why you have different
moods in different groups?
Why sometimes you're the star at a party and
sometimes you're the baby in the corner?
Some people draw you closer while some just
repel?
You choose to talk at times while you prefer to
let it pass at others?
You'd play dress up for a house lunch but land
up at a party in athleisure?

That's cause you're partly reserved, partly vocal,
Cause you're mentally global, verbally local,
And you're pretty hard to get
cause you're Ambi-social!

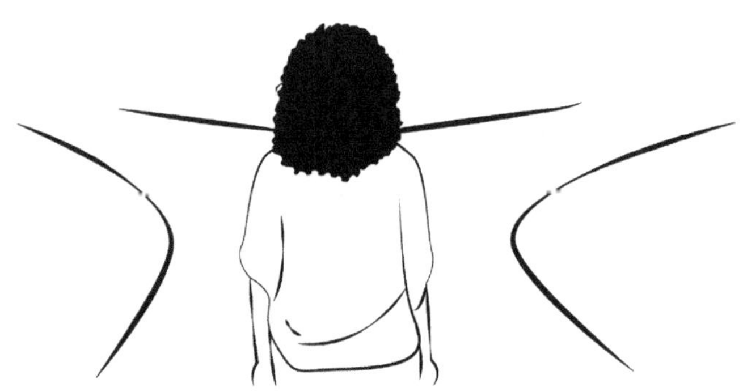

Disaster Chef

Just when you've got everything right and you
think you're a master,
A divine voice tells you to add some water and
you create a disaster.
The runny dough, the charred bread, the
undercooked rice,
The rocky cake, the salty curry or the overdose
of spice.
No matter how much I try, I am so culinarily
challenged—it's no joke.
No matter how many recipes I follow, my
endeavours end in a puff of smoke.

Let's just hope cloud kitchens and bread are
never out of vogue,
And God bless my cook with good health and no
more viruses go rogue.

'Growing Up'

The Year that Was

When we cut the cake for New Year, hardly did
we know,
The unprecedented way the coming year was
going to go.
When the demon began to rear its head, we were
shocked to discover,
It had not one but several—each more ghastly
than the other.
Anxiety, death, destruction, losses followed and
mankind stood in a quagmire,
We realised the hard way, it's life itself that you
ultimately desire.
The year that marks the turn of this world,
toward things that really matter,
Transcending various ruts, various myths of life
that it has managed to shatter.

The best learning is that you only live once so
live every moment of the day,
The year that was, has taught us to make the best
of life, in every way.

मेरे पास कपड़े बहुत हैं

मेरे पास कपड़े बहुत हैं

एक दिन सोचा की वो सारे कपड़े जिनसे बुरी यादें जुड़ी
हैं
... उन्हें हटा दूँ।

एक नया कुर्ता जिसे पहली बार पहना था,
उस दिन दफ्तर में गिरी थी, फिर छह महीने ठीक से
चल नहीं पाई थी
उस कुर्ते को देख कर उस दर्द की याद आती है
... इसलिए उसे हटा दूँ।

एक दुपट्टा जिससे ओढ़ कर माँ को अस्पताल में
देखने गई थी
बस आँख खोल कर उन्होंने मुझे एक बार देखा था
उस दुपट्टे को देख कर उस आख़िरी आंसू के बूँद की
याद आती है
... इसलिए उसे हटा दूँ।

एक शॉल भी था जिसे हरिद्वार की ठण्ड में लपेट रखा
था
सुबह पांच बजे अपने बचपन को पंचतत्व में विलीन
होते देखा था
उस शॉल को देख कर उस असीम खालीपन की याद
आती है
... इसलिए उसे हटा दूँ।

जब सारे कपड़े हटाए
सारी यादों को समेटा
फिर मुड़ कर देखा
तो पहनने के लिए कुछ बचा ही नहीं।

पर लोग अब भी कहते हैं
कि...मेरे पास कपड़े बहुत हैं।

Flawed and Beautiful

She fluttered in front of my eyes,
That beautiful streak of orange and black.
She stayed on a few flowers and leaves,
flew past me and kept coming back.
I tried to trace her with my eyes,
She was a whizzing speck in the sky.
She soared so high, I could hardly see her,
At times she made me wish I could fly.
For one brief moment, she glided towards me,
As if she had heard me calling out to her.
As I waited for her to come nearer
She turned and again became a blur.
She circled around the garden and sat on a
flower in one of the pots,
Her wings spread out in full glory,

blazing orange with charcoal black spots.
As I leaned in and focused on her, for a perfect
shot, inching closer,
She stood still, as I clicked, she was in fact quite
a poser.
Right when I was done with taking pictures, to
my delight,
She snapped out of her stance and disappeared
into the twilight.
Back inside the house, I skimmed through my
prized possessions,
Some had come out a little hazy but some
complete perfection.
I couldn't help but notice that the gorgeous thing,
Had a beautiful print on but also burns on one
wing.
She was blessed with beauty but life for her had
been rough,
While it hadn't been easy for her, she surely
seemed to be tough.
Life isn't fair, isn't easy, isn't all good,
But it's worth living to the fullest and we all
should.

And not every beautiful thing needs to be perfect
to leave you in awe,
Sometimes your beauty lies in the way you own
your flaw.

Champi Chats

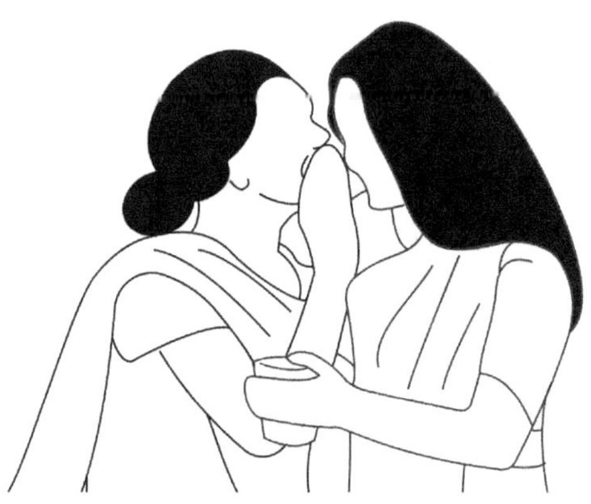

Every Saturday night, oiling your hair is a
family ritual.
In winters, this starts by warming up the oil and
as the oil loosens, so does the atmosphere.
Invariably your semblance of a maternal figure
starts by exclaiming how your hair needs more
care,
She runs her hands through your hair, at a
convenient height for this inspection and makes
further ungratifying diagnosis.
At an all-time low hair-morale, your saviour is
finally ready—
The glistening messiah like a genie in a bottle
set to give you ad-worthy hair.
As runnels of oil get soaked into your scalp and
soothe your mind like water mending dried-up

soil, it's time for champi and the conversation
begins—
Of the time when you were in college and the
boy you said was your friend.
Of that girl you met on the train and how she
became a model.
Of your batchmates in the States and whether
they're home for Christmas.
Of the friend you had said was expecting and
how she has been.
Of your plans at work, your closest friends, your
new ideas and how you need to embrace
changes as they come and go.
Of how being happy is the most important of all
things we aspire to be.
And finally, my hair is braided and just like the
conversation, ready to grow longer and stronger.
So, roles are reversed now and it's time for the
oil to be put on the greyer hair, the wiser head.

माँ

सब कहते होंगे दादी माँ, हम तो माँ ही कहते थे, उनके
दिल में हर हमेशा हम ही हम तो रहते थे।
चाहे शाम के चार बजे हो, या हो सुबह के चार,
उनको फोन लगाया हो तो उठाएंगी हर बार,
डर से नींद ना आए तब हम फोन लगाते थे,
जब तक नींद नहीं आ जाए तब तक वो गप्प सुनाते
थे।

खाना लेकर कॉलेज में वो लचं ब्रेक में आते थे,
हांथ धुलवाकर, मुँह पौंछ कर ही फिर वापस जाते थे।
चाहे जो हो इच्छा वो हमेशा पूरी करते थे,
पर ज़िद का साथ नहीं देते जो है ज़रूरी करते थे।

आज भी हर दिन कोई ना कोई बात उनकी याद
दिलाती है,
उनकी स्मृति हृदय को छूकर आँखों को छलकाती है।
उनके आशीर्वाद से अब आगे परिवार का हाथ थामना
है,
हो ऐसा ही प्रेम मेरे लिए भी, जीवन में यही कामना है।

Thank you, Hill View

Fifty shades of green and lovely colourful blooms,
Sungazing every morning through cozy, breezy rooms.
Delighted chirps of beautiful birds and calming sounds of nature,
The rarest plants and trees around, every house's regular feature.
The heavy iron gate that takes one's all just to move,
Above it a canopy of pink flowers swaying in their own groove.
The road strewn with flora, youngsters' popular photo point,

While in the evenings, for veteran walkers, it
becomes a catch-up joint.
The red bungalows, the tall arches and the high
ceiling,
All of them together give a vintage regal feeling.
Of all the places that I have called home, this
was closest to the heart,
The chatty family tea time gave the day a soulful
start.
Just the memory of Hill View Road makes the
heart fill up with good vibes,
Grateful for all the cherished moments it brought
into our lives.

'Older and Wiser'

Life's like that

It's really simple and still so layered,
So rough and yet so smoothened out.
It's stormy like the sea but also calm,
It's grainy like sand but also fine.
It's half-full of laughter and half-empty of tears,
It's all about moments and just about years.
It's not for the faint-hearted nor for the uptight,
It's for those who know it's worth, those who are
just right.
So make the most of it, make it your best one,
Cause there is just one life and retakes there are
none!

Forever friend

From teens to tweens to being drama queens, she
has always been mine,
Year after year, she has aged for the better, much
like the finest wine.

She held me close when life dealt me some of its
biggest blows,
And that there was a time I wanted to become a
heroine, only she knows.

Be it Cleopatra's eyes or stumbling over sarees,
we would giggle through it all,
Even while dozing off at each other's place we
always had a ball.

In Eco class, we would be caught smiling at
each other across the room,
During marching practice, we would gossip
about which boy was after whom.

After school, we parted ways but we grew closer
still,
Take Delhi, London, Bangalore, Chennai or
USA, if you will.

Through crushes, heartbreaks, love and life, we
have been each other's shoulder,
With time and tide though, she grew more
beautiful, wiser and even bolder.

Firgun females, we wish each other happiness of
every kind,
Be it day or night, we are always on each other's
mind.

Love and good vibes always for Bue, my forever
friend,
Hope and pray, unlike all good things our laugh
riots never end!

The Message

It's Saturday afternoon Netflix time,
The room is dark, the TV is bright,
The fan is on and the AC is right,
The water bottle is near and the remotes are in
sight,
The sofa is comfy but there's just one thing you
need for the perfect showtime cocoon—a
blanket.

So you tell the husband to get it from the room,
He looks at you and moves as if to get up.

You're stretching out in anticipation of the
incoming blanket,
And suddenly he picks up the remote and
switches off the AC,

Immediately the room starts to get warm and he
turns to you and gives a sly grin which says,

'If you no get up, nor will I,
let's thaw together and watch The Spy. '

Now, that's a message.

Tudum!

Sorted by Girth

For as long as I have known, I have always been
chubby,
They told me I will need to slim down to find
myself a hubby.
The weighing scale, the garment store, would
give me a nightmare,
The donuts on my dessert plate gave passersby a
scare.
No matter how well I did at Math, what mattered
was my growing bum,
Every body-shamer in the house would beat my
belly like a drum.
As time went by, my self-esteem grew to
discover,
Beauty is what lies in the book and not what's on
its cover.

Now I know that taunts and teasers do not
decide my worth,
Now I am sorted to love myself always—even
when sorted by girth.

Supermoms

They are just everywhere,
You know them, you see them,
And you also want to be them.

They can walk the talk,
They can block and stalk,
They can dress and impress,
They can feed and express.
They paint and read and have skincare routines,
They eat right, sleep nice and look like their
teens.

They can carry bumps with sky-high heels,
They wow clients and strike super deals.
Their idea of a workout is one kid on each arm,
They double up as shields to keep them away
from harm.

They dance to make their kids laugh and bake
nice stuff,
They smile to keep them happy even when
they've had enough.

Just how they do it all, to me, is a wonder,
They manage everything without even a blunder,
While they confess they are a mess in many
different ways,
I guess, that means, even Supermoms can have
their bad days.

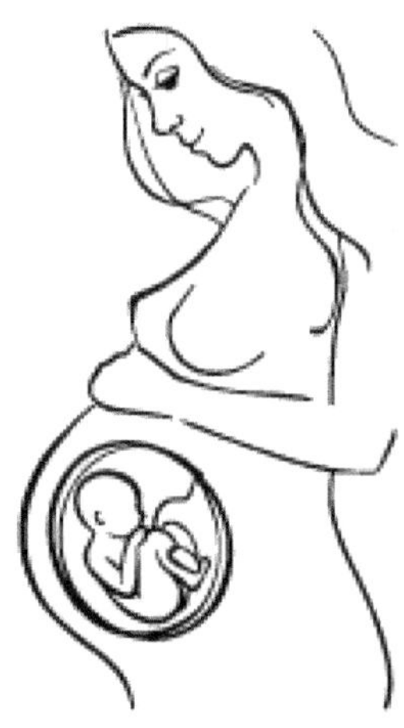

Madre

Every room she enters is lit with her booming
voice,
We love this sound of music while some may
call it noise.
Her radiant glow and warm smile can thaw
everything cold,
Her well-meaning banter woos all alike—young
or old.

When she's home we can't keep calm and when
she's not, we miss her,
When she's her loving self, we virtually kiss her.

When she talks we listen, when she laughs we
jump for joy,
Sometimes she's our Lara Croft, sometimes our
Helen of Troy.

Do what is right or you'll invoke her wrath,
She'll tell you off but also help you take the
right path.
She can be painfully honest even if it puts you in
a spot,
She is the OG badass whether you like it or not.

For her knowledge and wisdom, she is always
respected,
At times she understands you in ways you never
expected.
She spends sleepless nights for us and never
stops to think,
And when we are fine, she is fast asleep in a
blink.

She has the loudest laugh and a wicked sense of
humour,
She can keep a secret but can't resist spreading a
rumour.
She is our dearest treasure, we realise as we get
old,
She is our diamond while we are her gold.

Now that I am a mom, I love her even more,
I empathise with her like I never could before.
When I am clingy I call her Momma, Madre and
even Mother,
She's one of a kind, she's mine and like her, there
can be no other.

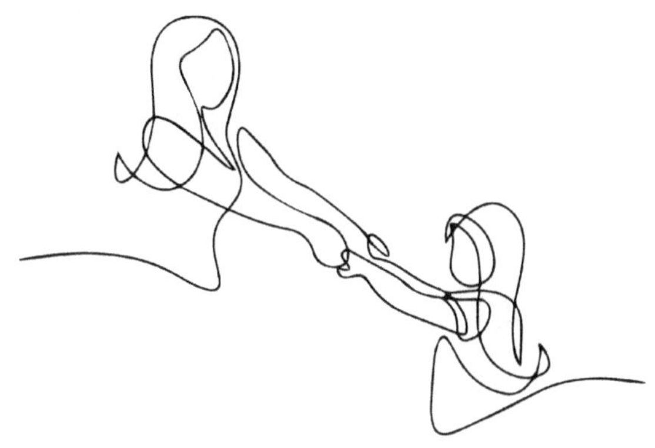